THE OVERLORD EMBROIDERY

THE MAKING OF THE EMBROIDERY

The Overlord Embroidery was the brainchild of Lord Dulverton of Batsford. He regarded the success of Operation OVERLORD as such an outstanding achievement that he resolved to commission his own personal tribute to all those involved. He conceived the Overlord Embroidery as a modern counterpart to the Bayeux Tapestry and, in 1968, chose a talented young artist, Sandra Lawrence, to design it.

For each panel Lawrence first prepared a 'thumbnail sketch' using wartime photographs for reference. The sketches were discussed by an advisory committee set up by Lord Dulverton to guide the making of the Embroidery. It included a retired senior officer from each of the services: Admiral Sir Charles Madden, General Sir Charles Jones and Air Chief Marshal Sir Donald Evans, collectively dubbed 'The Three Wise Men'. Once a sketch was approved, Sandra Lawrence painted a full size watercolour of it, one for each of the 34 panels. Using these designs, embroidered panels, each 2.4m long and 0.9m deep (8ft x 3ft), were created by the Royal School of Needlework. They began work by stretching strong cotton fabric onto a wooden embroidery frame. Purple crestweave linen was placed on top and the two layers sewn together.

Sandra Lawrence's designs were transferred to the linen using a technique which dates back to Tudor times, known as 'pricking and pouncing'. Hundreds of holes were pricked through the lines of tracings taken from the paintings, and fine black powder, or 'pounce', was rubbed through, leaving a trail of dots on the linen. The dots were joined up and pieces of material, matching the colours and shapes shown in the paintings, were sewn on to the linen to create the appliqué (applied) panels.

More than 50 different materials were used in the making of the Embroidery, and 320m of cording used to edge the various elements in the designs. Over a five year period, twenty embroiderers and five apprentices at the Royal School of Needlework worked to complete the Embroidery, which is 83m (272 ft) in length.

Lord Dulverton (1915–92), pictured in front of his family home, Batsford Park, Gloucestershire.

Sandra Lawrence in her studio, at work on the final panel of the Embroidery.

Margaret Bartlett, head of the workroom at the Royal School of Needlework, supervising the team of embroiderers at work on panel 32.

A detail from Sandra Lawrence's watercolour for panel 26, with the photograph which inspired her portrait of the German prisoner. The original watercolours were presented to the American government in 1994 and are on display in the Pentagon, Washington.

FACES OF THE FAMOUS

Visitors to the D-Day Museum find the likenesses of famous wartime personalities one of the most striking aspects of the Embroidery. Above is Vice-Admiral Mountbatten; below, the Prime Minister, Winston Churchill.

The faces were the work of Ruby Essam, an employee of the Royal School of Needlework for over 50 years. She worked them separately on a small square frame, using flesh-coloured material and a variety of flesh-toned embroidery threads in long and short stitch. As faces were completed, they were applied to the appropriate panels with final adjustments being made to ensure that each was instantly recognizable.

DISPLAYING THE EMBROIDERY

When the Overlord Embroidery was ready, Lord Dulverton arranged for it to tour exhibition sites in the USA and Canada. However, plans for it to go on permanent display at the Imperial War Museum fell through when planning permission for a new gallery to house it could not be secured. Instead the Embroidery went for a time to Edinburgh before going on display in the Porter Tun Room at the Whitbread Brewery in London in 1978.

Meanwhile Lord Dulverton continued his search for a permanent exhibition site, and this finally came to fruition in the lead-up to the 40th anniversary of D-Day in 1984. Portsmouth, which had been so closely involved in the mounting of Operation OVERLORD in 1944, was planning a small display to commemorate the anniversary. Hearing that the Overlord Embroidery was available, the city council offered to house it as part of a brand-new museum devoted to the Normandy landings. Lord Dulverton accepted Portsmouth's generous offer, and the museum was completed in just eight months.

The D-Day Museum was opened by HM Queen Elizabeth The Queen Mother on 3 June, 1984, with the Embroidery as its centrepiece. The Embroidery is displayed in specially designed and lit showcases, within a circular gallery maintained at a constant temperature and humidity. These conditions, together with the regular inspections that are carried out, should help to ensure that the longevity of the Embroidery will match that of the Bayeux Tapestry.

HM Queen Elizabeth The Queen Mother at the opening of the D-Day Museum in 1984.

Panel 30 (below), which shows the ruins of Caen, is the only panel which is the work of one embroiderer at the Royal School of Needlework. When the Embroidery was first completed in 1972, it consisted of 33 panels. Then, early in 1973, Lord Dulverton proposed that another panel should be added, dealing with the struggle for Caen. When Sandra Lawrence's watercolour was ready, however, the workroom at the Royal School was busy with a new commission. So one of the most experienced embroiderers, Wendy Hogg (right) worked the panel on her own. It took her six months to complete.

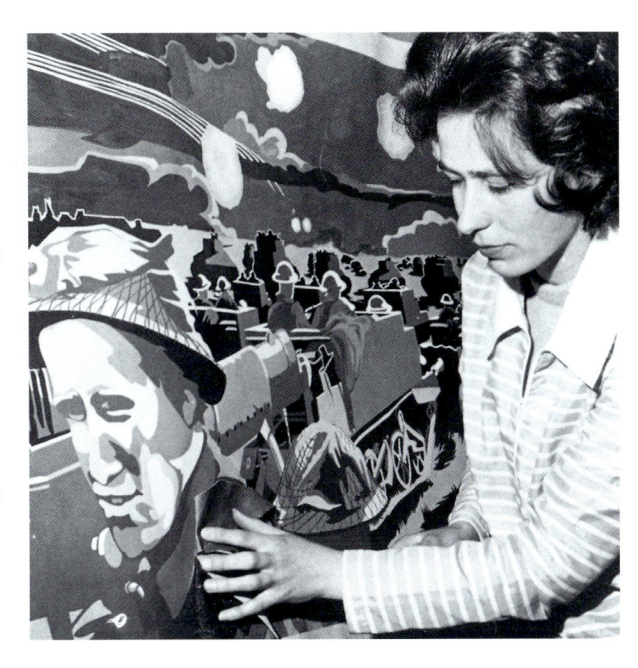

THE PIPER'S BERET

One of the highlights of the D-Day Museum's Soundalive guide to the Embroidery comes when visitors reach panel 17 and actually hear Piper Bill Millin (above) playing his pipes and describing the events of D-Day. In 1944 Millin was personal piper to Lord Lovat, commander of the 1st Special Service (Commando) Brigade. When panel 17 was first completed, Bill Millin was shown wearing a helmet. When he saw it, Piper Millin protested to Lord Dulverton that this was a mistake. The embroidered head was therefore sent back to the Royal School of Needlework, where the helmet was duly replaced by the green commando beret that Millin, like all Lovat's men, wore on D-Day.

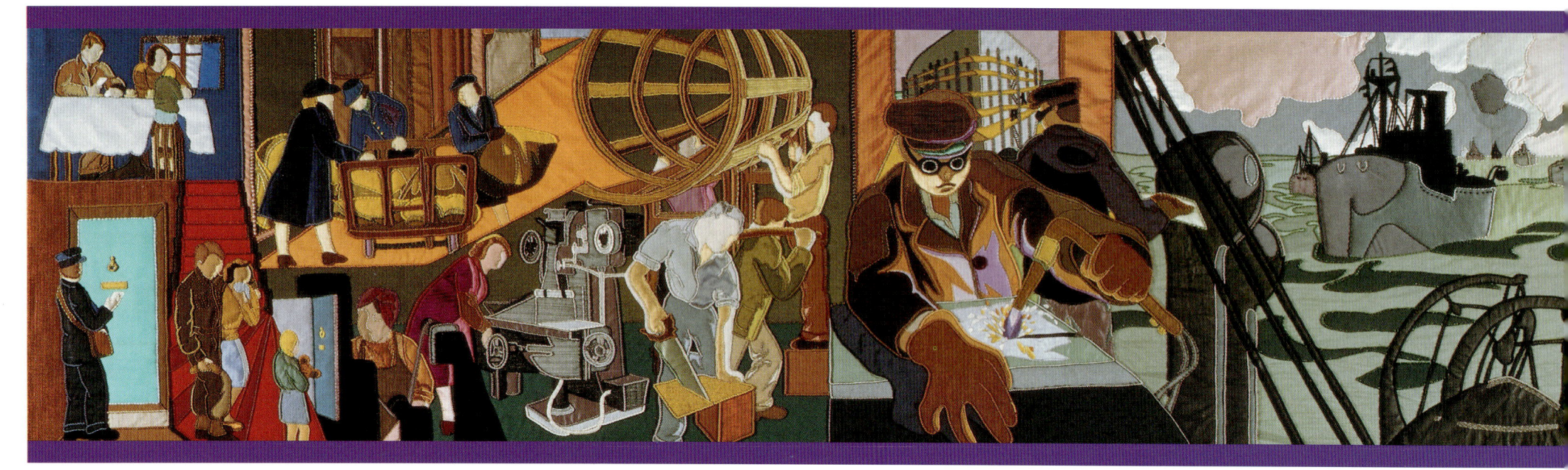

1 In 1940 Britain and the Commonwealth, fighting for survival and bereft of allies, save for the free forces of the nations conquered by Germany, begin the build-up of industrial and military strength to continue the war. A civilian receives his call-up papers; others build ships and aircraft; women, too, are employed in machine shops and on the railways. Convoys of merchant ships defy enemy submarines to maintain the flow of supplies to the shores of Britain.

3 The Blitz: from September 1940 to May 1941 the German Air Force concentrates its attacks on British cities. In London, where nearly 30,000 civilians are killed and many more lose their homes, people hasten to a tube station for shelter. Searchlight beams pick out the enemy bombers overhead and the guns of an anti-aircraft battery open fire. Civil Defence organizations – fire fighters and air raid wardens – deal with the fierce fires caused by the bombing; nurses tend the injured.

War production continues: tanks are built; Land Army girls go to work on the farms. Gas attacks are expected; children practise wearing their masks. During the Battle of Britain RAF Spitfires and Hurricanes take off to engage raiders in the struggle for command of the air, the loss of which forces Hitler to abandon his plans for invading England. The battle is directed from an underground operations room where girls of the Women's Auxiliary Air Force plot the position of the aircraft on a large map.

2

In the battle to keep open the Atlantic convoy routes, a destroyer of the Royal Navy depth-charges a German U-boat. Canadian sailors, who play an important part in this battle, arrive at a British port. The Home Guard, raised to help resist any invading Germans, learn arms drill with umbrellas and walking sticks, while they wait for weapons and uniforms to arrive. In December 1941 America declares war and by the Spring of 1942 US troops begin to assemble in the United Kingdom.

4

5

In the air offensive, RAF four-engined bombers attack German towns at night. Spitfires at the limit of their range clash with enemy fighters over the coast of Europe; formations of American Flying Fortress bombers raid industrial targets in daylight. The fighters return to refuel; bomber crews leave their aircraft after a raid.

6

Planning the return to Europe; Vice-Admiral Mountbatten, Chief of Combined Operations, and some of his staff devise special landing craft and armoured vehicles for amphibious landings. Soldiers are trained on assault courses and full-scale invasion exercises are held on the English coast.

7

In France, Field Marshal Rommel, the German commander responsible for the Channel coast, inspects the booby-trapped beach obstacles and fortified gun batteries forming the Atlantic Wall, which the Allies must breach. Many of the obstacles are designed by Rommel himself. British agents, landed by night by Lysander aircraft, bring arms and aid to the French Resistance, whose sabotage of bridges and railways helps to disrupt German communications.

8 Landing craft and ships of the Allied navies concentrate in assembly ports in southern England; many merchant seamen take part in the invasion, and they are represented here by the captain of a British tug. British paratroops are briefed and glider pilots trained. American troops queue for their rations at an assembly camp and Allied tanks move to the marshalling areas on the south coast of England, which for security purposes has been sealed off from the rest of the country.

10 Shortly before D-Day, the invasion forces, confined to their camps near the embarkation ports along the south coast of England, make last-minute preparations. An officer inspects a Royal Marine commando's equipment; General Montgomery, the Allied land forces commander, gives one of his many 'pep talks' to the troops; in the docks trucks are loaded aboard a merchant ship. King George VI inspects one of the RN crews about to take part in the invasion.

American Flying Fortresses and Marauders join Lancasters and Mosquitoes in attacking communications targets in France to isolate the intended invasion area. Airfields and coastal defences are also bombed. The supreme commander, General Eisenhower, discusses the OVERLORD plan with senior Allied commanders – Air Chief Marshal Tedder, Admiral Ramsay, Air Chief Marshal Leigh-Mallory and Generals Montgomery, Bradley and Bedell Smith.

9

There are only a few days in each month with the right conditions of tide and moon for the invasion. When bad weather delays the start of the operation by 24 hours, many of the troops are already embarked aboard their landing craft. Here troops of the British 3rd Division and 27th Armoured Brigade await the order to sail. Most of the soldiers are grim-faced, but three on the left find light relief in the guidebook to France specially prepared for the invasion forces.

11

12   13

On 5 June the weather forecast improves a little and the invasion convoys set sail, concentrating off the Isle of Wight before turning south towards the French coast. The armada is protected by 15 squadrons of Allied fighters. Destroyers and maritime aircraft search the Channel for hostile submarines and warships.

During the day the fleet moves slowly south towards the Normandy coast; some smaller craft sink in the rough water, others have to turn back. The armada, which includes some 4,200 landing ships and landing craft, is escorted by 1,200 warships. Also amongst this fleet are the blockships, called Corncobs, which will be sunk to form sheltered anchorages off the beaches. RAF Lancasters, which bomb the German coastal batteries in the early hours of D-Day, fly above the ships.

14

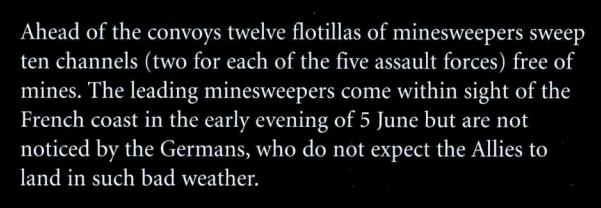

Ahead of the convoys twelve flotillas of minesweepers sweep ten channels (two for each of the five assault forces) free of mines. The leading minesweepers come within sight of the French coast in the early evening of 5 June but are not noticed by the Germans, who do not expect the Allies to land in such bad weather.

15

Shortly before midnight on 5 June the Allied airborne forces take off to capture vital bridges and gun batteries on the flanks of the invasion area. General Eisenhower talks to men of the US airborne divisions and British paratroops synchronize watches as gliders, in their black and white D-Day recognition markings, take off.

16

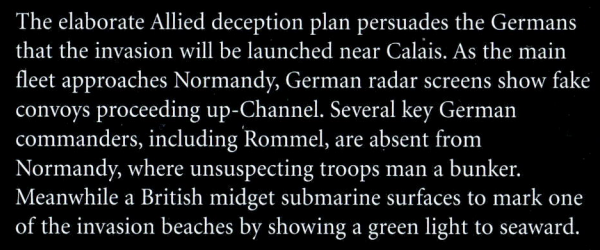

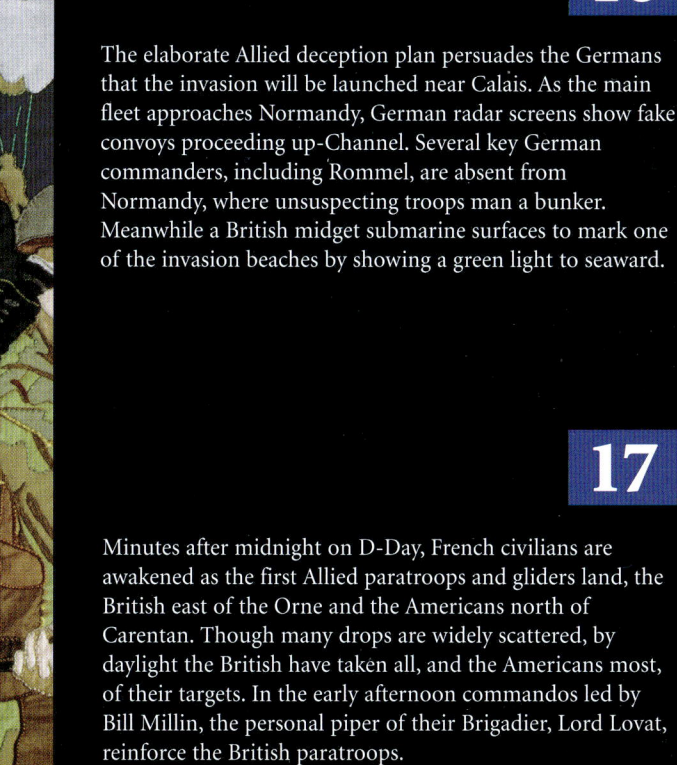

The elaborate Allied deception plan persuades the Germans that the invasion will be launched near Calais. As the main fleet approaches Normandy, German radar screens show fake convoys proceeding up-Channel. Several key German commanders, including Rommel, are absent from Normandy, where unsuspecting troops man a bunker. Meanwhile a British midget submarine surfaces to mark one of the invasion beaches by showing a green light to seaward.

17

Minutes after midnight on D-Day, French civilians are awakened as the first Allied paratroops and gliders land, the British east of the Orne and the Americans north of Carentan. Though many drops are widely scattered, by daylight the British have taken all, and the Americans most, of their targets. In the early afternoon commandos led by Bill Millin, the personal piper of their Brigadier, Lord Lovat, reinforce the British paratroops.

18 Shortly before dawn on D-Day the invasion forces assemble off the Normandy coast: the Americans to the west, the British and Canadians to the east. Despite the prevailing rough weather, the Channel crossing has been accomplished without serious loss or interference by the enemy. Tank landing craft begin to launch amphibious DD (duplex drive) tanks, fitted with large canvas screens to buoy them up, and propellers to enable them to 'swim' ashore.

20 After the aerial bombardment of the invasion beaches, the heavy guns of navy ships open fire over a 50 mile (80km) front on selected targets such as coastal batteries. Allied naval forces include 7 battleships, 2 monitors, 23 cruisers and 103 destroyers. A Mustang flies over the fleet, reporting to the naval gunners on the accuracy of their shooting, and giving information on new targets. In the background a Sunderland flying boat of RAF Coastal Command keeps watch.

As H-Hour approaches, the troops, cold and drenched with spray, many of them seasick, wait for the moment when the ramps go down. But many of the amphibious tanks have been launched too far out and are swamped or damaged in collisions. On Omaha beach, out of 32 DD tanks only 5 survive. Elsewhere the DD tanks are carried straight onto the beaches by the landing craft. Where they do go ashore, they give invaluable support to the infantry.

19

As the first assault waves head for the shore, the German coastal defence system is repeatedly attacked by British and American bombers. Before dawn Lancasters, Halifaxes and Mosquitoes bomb the beach defences and in daylight further attacks are made by American Flying Fortresses, Liberator and Marauder aircraft. The Allied air forces fly 14,674 sorties over the beaches on D-Day against 319 by the Luftwaffe. Allied mastery of the air is vital to the success of OVERLORD.

21

22 At H-Hour, which varies from beach to beach according to the state of the tide, the five Allied assault divisions hit the shore. On Utah beach, a lucky mistake in navigation brings the leading assault craft in about a mile (1.5km) further south than intended, where the German defences are weak. 4th US Division, supported by 28 amphibious tanks, loses less than 350 men in the landings and is soon pressing inland to link up with the airborne troops.

24 Then it is the turn of the British and Canadians to head for the beaches in their assault landing craft (LCAs), with Mosquitoes and Thunderbolts shown flying overhead. The assault divisions storm ashore on their three beaches: 50th Northumbrian Division, with its double-T formation badge, on Gold; 3rd Canadian Division on Juno; 3rd British Division on Sword. The tide rises rapidly, covering the mined obstacles and causing congestion on the beaches, but the German defences are soon overcome.

On Omaha beach the going is far tougher for 1st US Division. Many landing craft sink, as do most of the amphibious tanks which are launched. The troops are pinned down by concentrated fire from a seasoned German division, and are forced to shelter behind Rommel's beach obstacles. But the courage and experience of 1st US Division, supported by gunfire from destroyers coming close inshore, eventually enables the Americans to establish a slim beachhead at the cost of 3,000 casualties.

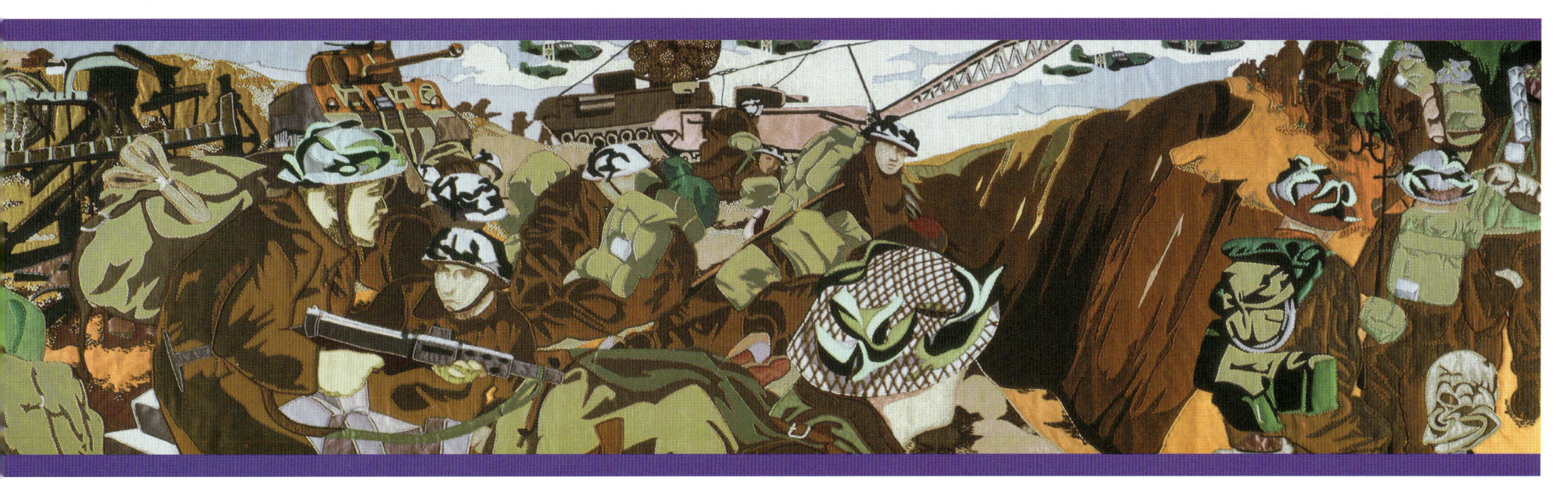

23

The British and Canadian assault is greatly helped by the success of the 79th Armoured Division's 'funny' tanks, specially designed to tackle the German defences of the Atlantic Wall. These include flail tanks with chains to beat paths through German minefields, tanks with bundles of brushwood to fill in ditches, and bridging tanks to cross other obstacles. The troops, still hoping to use the bicycles with which they were issued, push inland as Mustangs fly overhead on armed reconnaissance.

25

26 After D-Day the Allied bridgehead in Normandy is gradually expanded. Here American troops move inland across the area flooded by the Germans and begin the battle to cut the neck of the Cotentin peninsula. German resistance is overcome and many prisoners are taken. US B-26 Marauders fly overhead to attack German forces trying to move up to the front. On the left an amphibious tank, its canvas flotation screen lowered, has been knocked out.

28 King George VI visits the invasion beaches on 16 June and Winston Churchill and Field Marshal Brooke on 12 June. In this panel they are shown together with Generals Eisenhower and Montgomery. In the background, ships unload stores in the prefabricated Mulberry harbour at Arromanches. Consisting of old ships, massive concrete blocks and floating roadways, this extraordinary construction was one of the great feats of wartime engineering.

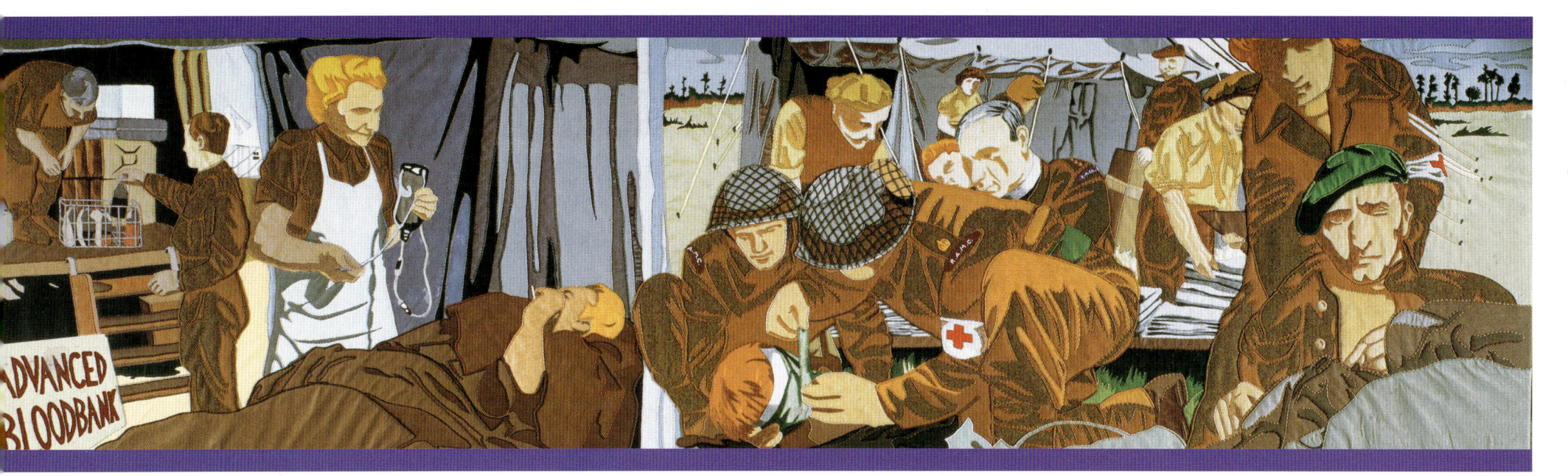

Prompt treatment and modern medical techniques – notably blood transfusions and new drugs – reduce the number of fatal casualties on D-Day and during the months of fighting which follow. Here nurses, doctors and orderlies of the Royal Army Medical Corps tend the wounded at an Advanced Dressing Station at the front and in a Field Hospital behind the lines. Severe cases are soon taken to hospitals in England. A Chaplain helps and comforts an injured man.

27

In June and July the Allies fight to enlarge their bridgehead. The fighting is bitter; in the close Normandy countryside – the *bocage* – the German tanks and guns are advantageously placed in strong defensive positions behind thick hedges and banks. Repeated offensives draw the German armoured forces to the British sector, particularly in the area of Caen, enabling the Americans in the west, with much hard fighting, to prepare for a decisive breakthrough.

29

30

Caen is not taken on D-Day and its capture remains essential to the development of the campaign. Preceded by a dusk attack by Halifaxes and Lancasters of Bomber Command and accompanied by massed artillery, air and naval gunfire support, 1st British Corps attack in the early hours of 8 July. On 9 July 3rd British and 3rd Canadian Divisions meet in the city. But the bridges over the Orne have been blown and for another ten days the Germans command the through routes to the south and east.

31

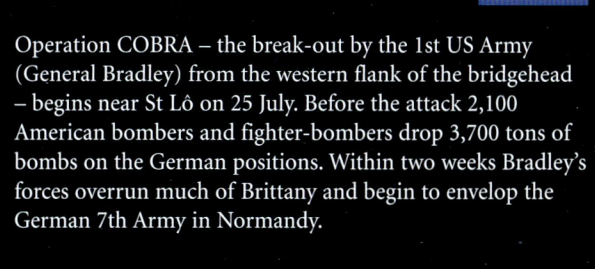

Operation COBRA – the break-out by the 1st US Army (General Bradley) from the western flank of the bridgehead – begins near St Lô on 25 July. Before the attack 2,100 American bombers and fighter-bombers drop 3,700 tons of bombs on the German positions. Within two weeks Bradley's forces overrun much of Brittany and begin to envelop the German 7th Army in Normandy.

32

To complete this envelopment, 1st Canadian Army begins a southward offensive – Operation TOTALIZE – towards Falaise on 7 August. Coloured smoke and streams of tracer shells guide the armoured columns into the attack, which is made under cover of darkness and preceded by heavy bombing of enemy positions. Improvised armoured personnel carriers (tanks without their turrets) carry infantry into the assault.

33 In mid-August the German 7th Army, whose westward counter-attack towards Mortain fails to dislodge the Americans, is trapped by the Allied armies in a salient known as the Falaise Pocket. In the subsequent action 10,000 Germans are killed and 50,000 captured. Rocket-firing Typhoons are shown attacking enemy transport and armour. On the left is shown a tank of 1st Polish Armoured Division whose troops play a notable part in the operation.

34 Defeated in Normandy, the Germans retreat across the River Seine towards the Belgian border. In many French towns, including Paris, the inhabitants rise against the German garrisons. In this panel a Frenchman, suspected of being a member of the Resistance movement and shot by the retreating Germans, is discovered by his relatives as a British infantry platoon marches by. France is within sight of early liberation, but the Allies face eight more months of bitter fighting before Germany is finally overcome.